HOME SERIES

HOME SERIES
COSMOPOLITAN LIVING

BETA-PLUS

CONTENTS

P. 4-5
A Minus project in a house
created by architect Tom
Vanbiervliet.

P. 6
Cosmopolitan style in this 85
square metres loft designed by
Bruno Van Besien.
The existing brick walls were
retained and painted white to
make the space as light as
possible, in contrast with the
solid character of the building.

INTRODUCTION

 or many people, a home in a big city means a refuge from the hectic rhythm and stress that are all part of cosmopolitan life.

Whether the featured property is a simply designed loft, a cosily furnished hôtel de maître, a designer flat or a luxurious townhouse, the intention is always to create a unique haven that has been built or adapted to accomodate the lifestyle and character of the owners.

This lavishly illustrated book features extensive reports about the ultimate in city living.
These are unique snapshots of what well-known interior architects see as the ideal modern city home: light and spacious, inviting or escapist, sober or exuberant, with most of the projects involving a strong focus on contemporary art and design.

P. 8
An Yvonne Hennes project (by PHYL).
A table and tabouret from Maxalto (Simplice collection). The two armchairs are also from Maxalto (Apta collection). Lamps by Piet Boon, model Klaar. Artworks by Han Lei, "Fictional Portraits".

P. 10-11
An interior design project by Ensemble & Associés (architect Gregory Dellicour, wood construction Mi Casa). The L-shaped living room is oriented around the hearth and library wall, entirely finished in sandblasted, black stained oak. The hearth-fire (on bio-ethanol) limits the TV-corner.

LONDON CALLING

F ormally utilised to sell apartments in the Barbican Estate, the Estate Office remained empty for ten years before being purchased by its new owners. On first inspection, the Estate Office with its unusual spatial volumes, architectural elements and raw materials, was seen as a treasure that would make a remarkable central London home.

Both clients, Ken Mackay and Tracey Wiles, are practising architects. Ken runs his own practise, Mackay + Partners and Tracey is a designer at Make Architects.

The design approach was clear, to preserve the existing structure, the various spatial volumes and raw materials with minimal intervention of new building work.

The original 420 m^2 footprint over two levels was increased by portioning off a 70 m^2 one bedroom flat (later sold on) to the upper floor and injecting a mezzanine floor, to form the master suite, creating the 350 m^2 home.

A success of the apartments' layout revolves around the interconnected spatial volumes. Narrow and tall spaces link with long and low spaces all of which surround the communal lift and stair core penetrating the centre of the apartment. The spatial character and the unusual sequence of spaces are so strong that the building dictated the allocation of use. The internal plan was penned after the initial viewing of the property and was not altered since.

P. 14-15
New front doors in Corten steel blend seamlessly with the brick façade and open onto the main living space. Storage areas either side of the entry, form a library and wine cellar servicing the lounge and dining areas. The two storey space is impressively framed by massive concrete columns and slot windows allowing sunlight to dramatically streak through the space.

A charcoal grey lacquer wall forms a backdrop to the kitchen bench and integrated dining area. The space, in contrast to the lofty height of the living space, is long and low and is also framed by the concrete columns and slot windows.

Flanking the central concrete core to one side is a small secondary corridor serving the two children's rooms. On the opposite side is a two metre wide and five metre high corridor punctuated with a leather padded room inserted into a brick alcove. The two corridors connect the main living space to the heart of the building.

The mezzanine space provides an 80 m^2 master suite with study area, sleeping area, and a bathroom pod. The pod separates the living, bathing and dressing areas without touching the existing concrete structure.

FEELING AT HOME

IN A BRUSSELS OFFICE

his office created by Ensemble & Associés is ideally situated on the top floor of an apartment building in the heart of Brussels: a haven of calm in the capital.

A photographic mosaic by Robert Silvers. All the panelling was designed by Ensemble & Associés and finished in sandblasted and black stained larch.

A sofa by Poltrona Frau and armchairs by Casamilano. The coffee table was designed by Ensemble & Associés and realised in sandblasted, black stained larch.

P. 28-29
The library was designed by
Ensemble & Associés and finished
in sandblasted, black stained larch.
A work of art by Mac Cullum.

Office accessories in black crocodile leather. A work of art by Katya Legendre.

P.30
Miniature of a work created by Pal
Horvath in the northerly space.

P.32-33
A desk designed by Jean Nouvel for
Bulo and desk chairs by Charles Eames.

A COSMOPOLITAN APARTMENT

P ascal van der Kelen has been one of the leading architects and interior designers of his generation for several years.

As well as his own customised architecture and interior designs, he has also recently unveiled his own Home Collection.

This apartment shows how Pascal van der Kelen combines bespoke work, made using the architect's drawings, with elements from his Home Collection.

This collection includes a wide range of light fittings alongside a kitchen, seating furniture, beds and libraries.

The most commonly used materials are bog oak, enamelled glass, synthetic panels and leather, painted metal…

The apartment consists of two floors.

Plinth and rear wall made from black lava rock, in harmony with the painted bookshelves.
The bar furniture is hidden to the right of the television. There is a thin cushion on the plinth in the same leather as the coffee table. A bespoke wool carpet. The low table from the Home Collection by Pascal van der Kelen is made with a frame from polished stainless steel with a leather surface.

Seating furniture by Minotti with the frame in polished stainless steel and covered with grey flannel (for the long bench) and cognac-coloured leather (all single seats). All frame finishing in wooden strips.

The kitchen from the Home Collection by Pascal van der Kelen, here finished with front lower cupboards in enamelled glass, work surface with synthetic panels, and storage cupboards in bog oak.

Table and ceiling lamp from the Home Collection by Pascal van der Kelen: the table frame in polished stainless steel with bog oak surface, the lamp is a hanging structure made from polished stainless steel with a shade made in brown smoked and frosted glass. Bespoke wool carpet.

The parents' bedroom. Bed and headboard from the Home Collection by Pascal van der Kelen. The bed is made from bog oak and white flannel for the headboard with bedside cabinets painted in off-white gloss.

The master bathroom is designed completely from drawings by the architect and finished with grey lava rock and grey smoked glass for the sliding doors. Mirror and paintwork for the storage cupboards.

The shower room is next to the children's bedroom and is fully finished in natural stone from drawings by the architect. The continuous mirror that reaches the ceiling effectively doubles the space.

The parents' dressing room is situated between the bedroom and the bathroom and is fully customised from drawings by the architect. On the left the fronts are made from lacquer ware, on the right in grey smoked glass.

A 1960'S APARTMENT

WITH SEA VIEW

The challenge for this apartment from the 1960's: creating an oasis of calm and wellbeing, with a sea view.

Purity, light and restraint were the key words in this project by Ensemble & Associés.

The living room with sofas by Luz Interiors faces the sea.

A Luz Interiors desk and a chair designed by Charles Eames.

P. 48-49
The pure designed open space with
living room / kitchen / dining room.
The custom-made work was
designed by Ensemble & Associés.
A bio-ethanol fireplace.

The kitchen was finished in grooved, white varnished MDF. Work surface and wall in Negro Tebas composite stone.

The master bedroom opens out onto a terrace. The furniture was custom designed by Ensemble & Associés. A Charly chair by Luz Interiors.

The guest room. Custom design by Ensemble & Associés.

The joinery in the children's room was also designed by Ensemble & Associés.

All bathrooms and shower rooms were finished in the same style to continue the austere whole. 5X5 tiling for floors and walls. Joinery in grooved MDF and varnished white. Plumbing fittings from RVB.

A SOPHISTICATED,

CONTEMPORARY LIVING SPACE

A DP Architects (Patrycja Zac-zynska and Chris Schroder) is an internationally renowned architecture firm with offices in Poland and the UK.

They were awarded the task of designing a sophisticated, contemporary living space in a traditional building in the centre of London.

By using top quality, natural materials, elegant furniture and a passion for details ADP succeeded in creating a glamorous and yet timeless whole.

The existing layout was simplified: two small bedrooms made way for a spectacular living room and annexed dining area. The generous ceiling height – reinforced by the wall high library and kitchen cupboards – ensure that this apartment seems twice as big...

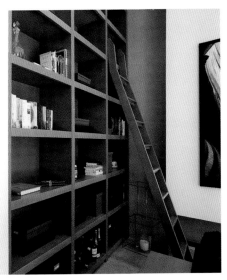

Rest and harmony in the living room, with two charcoal coloured sofas. The original, decorative windows are the only classical element in this contemporary living environment.
The potential of the high spaces was used optimally. Ladders give access to the highest library and kitchen cupboards.

Central on the left page, an African drum used as a vase.

P. 64-65
All the audio was hidden behind
the walls, the TV-screen was
integrated in the wall panel.

Simplicity and restraint in the bedroom but yet a warm and intimate feel through the soft fabrics in earthen shades.

The shower was given a central place in the bathroom.

SURROUNDED BY NATURE,

BUT VERY COSMOPOLITAN

T his house created by the architect Bruno Erpicum is limited at the entrance side to a single level, it is weightless on the water area that separates it from the entrance avenue. To the left, the entrance shows its gallery wall. Descending a level, the construction frames the view over the field, the countryside is yours.

To the left, behind you, a series of levels interrupted by stairs that stretch outside bring the profile of the site together. To the right, beyond the overhanging part that covers the dining room, the kitchen benefits from a lateral patio that bathes in the morning sun.

Go down further, the garden continues right up to the old trees in front of a swimming pool that is so long that it takes the liberty to fold back into the building through the fault-line freed up under the built-up framework.

Photo art works delivered by Artphotoexpo New York and Absolute Art Gallery. Furniture: InStore.

Four bedrooms complemented with an office on the mezzanine are arranged at the +1 level, the apartment of the owners is organized higher up on the roof, in a vast room devoid of partitions to make the bedroom into a covered terrace when the weather is good. Here, the heart is in the stars.

URBAN PENTHOUSE

T he Brion Leclercq (Julie Brion & Tanguy Leclercq A.D.) agency realised the interior layout of an urban penthouse located in Brussels.

Taking the glazed surface into account, they opted to divide the remaining walls in two in order to integrate the utility functions of the apartment and thereby opened up the living space to all visual angles.

All the storage is built into the panelling, which allows a fluidity of the movement and the living spaces.

The placement of the furniture and the creation of the panelling designed by the interior architects Julie Brion and Tanguy Leclercq made it possible to build in all the main functions in this apartment as well as the ventilation and air-conditioning facilities. The paintings shown are by the artist Sanam Khatibi.

Always with the desire to make the ambiance uniform and smooth, the architectural idea for the bathrooms consisted of choosing a limited range of materials and, in particular, using a simple material in multiple forms.

A large art deco polished steel mirror designed by the interior architects conceals the various storage areas in the bathroom.

A CONTEMPORARY

MAISON DE MAÎTRE

This private mansion in the heart of Antwerp dates from the end of the nineteenth century. The property has suffered over the years from the changing use and numerous renovations and modifications.

Hans Verstuyft Architects restored the residence in a contemporary and respectful way: a renewing approach but yet not forming a break with the past.

Materials and colours were used consistently that made the original architecture visible and emphasised it. Other additions (new floors, light fittings, etc.) were custom designed by the architect and seamlessly integrated into the authentic whole.

The interior was planned soberly; new elements are based on what might once have been there.

The new floors were laid with a natural stone framework. In this way they refer to the parquet and mosaic floors of the past.

Furniture and lighting were custom designed by Hans Verstuyft. The work surfaces in saddle leather have a magnificent patina.

The kitchen with the large fireplace and the loggia by the garden is a wonderful space in which many hours can be spent. Here everything has also been designed by the architect.

The cloakroom was designed a little more mysteriously and is thereby given an intimate character.

The bathroom is given a classic touch with the use of Carrara marble and dark wood. The link to the past can also be felt here.

Bedroom and dressing room were furnished exclusively with loose elements. The spatiality was maximally preserved as a result.

The children's bathroom was given a
fresh, young look: everything is white.

VERTICAL WALK

T he garden that separates the main part of the house is south facing, the bottom of the plot presents a level area that ends 6 metres higher up.

These are the only constraints to guide the architect Bruno Erpicum, who designed a residence based on two rings: a vertical ring ensures the connection between the levels, a horizontal ring includes the earth pressure at the rear and forms the interface between the main part and the rooms on the first floor. Everything is designed so as not to have to reveal the intimacy of the premises to passers-by, in this way, only a small section of the South facing garden is reserved to welcoming visitors and the entrance to the garage. To the right, the site climbs. Steps lead you to two levels in the area bathed in light... the upper garden. The vertical wall folds round to form the ceiling; it covers the living space which is simply organized around a white service area. The floor is black, it moves outside to the south, to form a vast patio. Three vertical circulations have been organised: the hall stairs, the lift and the family stairs that pierce the volume to the swimming pool.

All furniture has been delivered by InStore, the Brussels design interior shop.

All art work in this house has been delivered by Absolute Art Gallery and Artphotoexpo.

The view overhangs the neighbours so only the tops of the trees can be seen, two birches perforate the vertical patio encircled by the screen wall that makes the night-time areas on the lower level concealed from public view. The bedrooms and office situated in the depth are completed by their own patio.

Each time of the day has its own living framework, and one is never bored.

A CONTEMPORARY SEASIDE VILLA

Interior architect Marie-France Stadsbader transformed these semi-detached houses on the coast into a cosy weekend home for a young family. Despite the limited surface each function was still given its space.

The garage was converted into a spacious and practical living kitchen with custom made cupboards made from painted MDF, combined with a stainless steel work surface made by Obumex.

The dining room and living room are combined in one room but are still separated by a central supporting wall. All the walls are painted white to bring in as much light as possible combined with a few young, fresh touches of colour.
Chairs by Arne Jacobsen are placed around the dining table by Maarten Van Severen.

In the living room there is a coffee table by Poul Kjaerholm, a cupboard by Maarten Van Severen a standing lamp by Arco and a Flexform sofa.

The top floor is monochrome white: all the spaces are designed in the same way to form a single whole. White walls combined with a white painted parquet and fun objects ensure a pleasant living environment.

There is a Cappellini bed in the parents' bedroom and a chair by Hans Wegner and a magnificent Boffi fan as an alternative to air-conditioning in the summer.

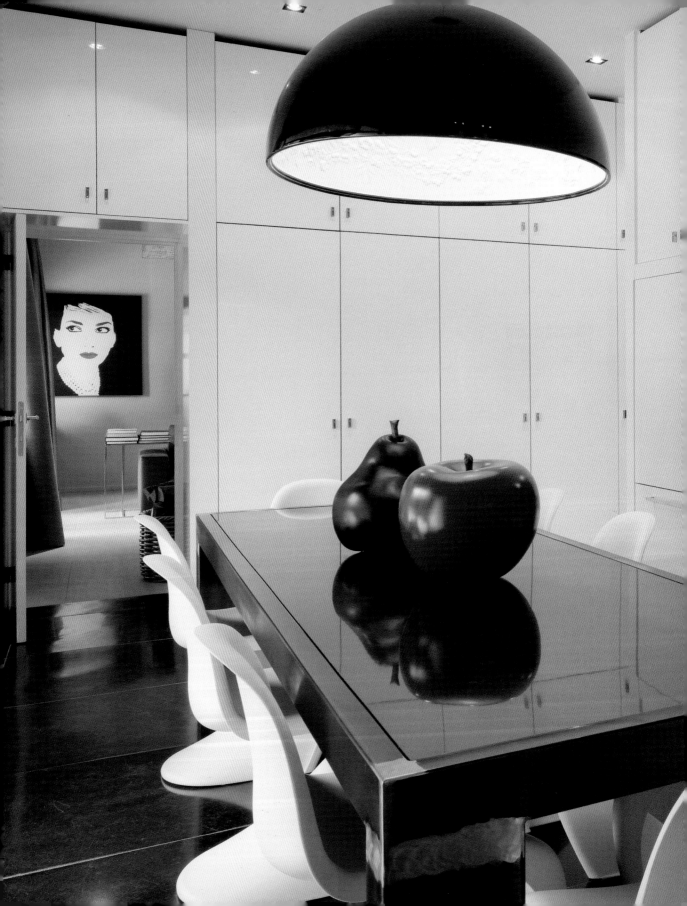

HOME SERIES

Volume 29 : COSMOPOLITAN LIVING

The reports in this book are selected from the Beta-Plus collection of home-design books: www.betaplus.com
They have been compiled in a special series by Le Figaro in French language: Ma Déco

Copyright © 2010 Beta-Plus Publishing / Le Figaro
Originally published in French language

PUBLISHER
Beta-Plus Publishing
Termuninck 3
B – 7850 Enghien
Belgium
www.betaplus.com
info@betaplus.com

PHOTOGRAPHY
Jo Pauwels

DESIGN
Polydem - Nathalie Binart

TRANSLATIONS
Txt-Ibis

ISBN: 978-90-8944-083-9

Printed in China

P.126-127
A kitchen project by Alexander
Cambron and Fabienne Dupont.